Her Name is SHE

Dr. Stephanie Helms Pickett

Dr. Stephanie Helms Pickett

Published by CaryPress

www.CaryPress.com

ISBN: 1631030019
ISBN-13: 978-1-63103-001-7

CaryPress and the logo are trademarks belonging to CaryPress.

PRINTED IN THE UNITED STATES OF AMERICA

DEDICATION

This work is dedicated to the she we are each becoming by the utility of SHE.

"Forsake her not, and SHE shall preserve thee: love her, and SHE shall keep thee." (Proverbs 4:6)

CONTENTS

ACKNOWLEDGMENTS

Thank you Heavenly Father, for seeing the need beyond this "she" and loving her despite what she projects, who she has rejected and who she is yet to become! Thank you for grace and unmerited favor and the opportunity to begin each day with newness forsaking the residue of yesterday. As a lover of words, I am sufficiently depleted of language to fully express my love for you.

To my husband Charles, you continue to support me, even when I don't fully support myself. Thank you for loving every "she" that shows up in different forms and finding the humor in each one. Thank you for sharing this journey with me and I pray that God continues to keep us knitted together and continues to bless our union and our blending family. To CJ, as you grow and God blesses you to meet and eventually wed one of his precious daughters, may you treat her as Christ treats the church and gave himself for it. To Niani, may you love our sisters through their projected pain, and may you love and appreciate yourself as God does. Mom, thank you for being a woman who loves and fears God, a woman of integrity, a woman of her word and a woman who is able to admit fault as well as forgive.

Thank you to my brother Marcus, sister Beverly, my aunts, cousins and friends near and far for supporting me to write, and encouraging others to support this living, ever evolving dream. You are most appreciated and celebrated.

I thank God for my Pastor J.J. Wilkins, Jr., and First Lady Cheryl Wilkins for their leadership and cultivating a place of worship and refuge at Wake Chapel Church in Raleigh, North Carolina. To my church family and the Anointed Soles Dance Ministry, thank you for your love and demonstration of faith and trust in God despite what the natural eye beholds.

Much love to my sisters at the Jaxton Creative Group for direction, clarity and innovation on this project. Thank you for Durdana at CaryPress for assisting in this project and the connection we experienced immediately in talking about the desire we share for our daughters to have healthy and happy relationships with women.

Thank you to Stephanie Henderson, Kieshia Cobb, Shavelle Bell, Kimberly McCrae, Kay Lewis, AY Bryant and Melcina White for their sisterhood and for allowing me a space to process this project with Godly wisdom.

Finally, this book was created to inspire conversation and purposeful action. Please take time to respond to the #SheWerk sections. Plan time and space to meet up with another sister (seasoned or lightly flavored) to laugh, love and share your responses. SHE compels you to do so! She will be blessed as a result, and so will you!

FOREWORD

"Teacher, which is the greatest commandment in the Law?" Jesus replied: "Love the Lord your God with all your heart and with all your soul and with all your mind." This is the first and greatest commandment. And the second is like it: "Love your neighbor as yourself." (Matthew 22:36-39)

She is my neighbor. At the appointed time our paths cross, I'm accountable for how I treat her. To love her as myself is to remove the grip of hatred, jealousy, malice, fear, and shame I feel in her presence. The enemy has convinced us that if she is ignored, we can maintain our position, power, and visibility. If that were true, our daughters, the next generation, wouldn't be so confused about what real love is. The enemy is a liar! God is love and he knows the power of it (John 3:16). Loving your neighbor is a command. Raising two girls who became drama queens in the 5th grade, it was important to show them how to love, encourage, and find beauty in all females. Often I explained, "You don't know her story, so don't judge and hate." Now it brings great joy and pride to hear them say to her, "I like your hair...I like your outfit...I like your make-up," especially if she's a complete stranger. She is often caught off guard receiving a compliment from another female who is expressing admiration and not ignoring her presence. As women, we can either be like Leah and Rachel in the book of Genesis, only seeing each other in terms of having something the other one wants, or like Elizabeth and Mary in the book of Matthew, rejoicing together because God has chosen us for something great.

I love being in my husband's Sunday School class. One morning he ended the lesson by saying, "let's empty ourselves before the Lord." I felt that statement was for me. For years I've been asking God to remove some past hurt and at that moment, I realized I could empty it, and let it go! I don't have to carry or wear it like a shirt. I can let it go! Once I said, "Lord I empty my fears, insecurities, trusting issues, etc.," I felt the woman he created me to be move into position. There was a lifting of heaviness as I walked into an environment that normally frustrated me.

We have to empty everything (withholding nothing) to truly love others and ourselves. She will either reveal the areas I need to empty or remind me that I am blessed and highly favored (sometimes both). I praise God for her! I need her. She is my neighbor.

Minister Melcina Yancey White

Shecessional

I've always loved her. As far back as I can remember, her impression on my life was captivatingly sound. Her motives genuine, loving and concerned for my well being. Even when we disagreed, the affection we shared was greater and more significant than the temporary gulf. In the event the disagreement persisted, and a third party was invited to assist in mediation, it was typically prayer or our collective memory that boldly reminded us our sisterhood was greater than our perceived disparity. We were determined not to allow something so insignificant to get in the way of our relationship. After all, we were the keepers of each other's secrets; we were the protectors of each other's dreams; we were the shelter for each other's storms; we were the accountability for each other's mistakes; and we were the bond for each other's brokenness. I was ying to her yang – and even though we each possessed distinct gifts, talents, faults and greatness – I would forever be brought back to center because I was her. I cared for her. I understood her. I celebrated her. And her I. Ours was a timeless interaction and could only be temporarily interrupted by life's challenges, rarely for long, and if so, never intentional, easily explained and quickly forgiven. After all, how could I afford to lose someone so precious who could make a mint auctioning off my life's drama on social media alone?

Sharing space with her was purposeful and it gave me life. Our interactions were deepened through connections, cultivated, navigated, negotiated and manifested in school, family, home, church, community and later in college and in the workplace. However, I was also afforded glimpses of her in the grocery store, riding public transportation, working in the dining hall, walking in my neighborhood, and even on television. Her smile of assurance warmed my heart as we stood next to each other in public spaces, or sat next to each other in the "sick baby" area of the pediatrician's office. Her embrace while passing the peace during Sunday service was sometimes the only one I'd received all week. I was grateful to her for the gesture extended by holding the door for me as I traveled with my arms full, or laughter for showing up at an event with the same dress. Yes, whether elongated or brief, hers and mine was that of a mutually exclusive experience.

Just before our happily ever after, a new person emerged. She looked like her. She showed up in similar spaces as her. Yet there was something different. She didn't walk or talk like what I recognized or was accustomed to. There was no familiarity of warmth in her eyes. As I searched for the commonality, I quickly realized there was greater than six degrees of separation between us. She made it clear that her relationship with me was only desired if I outwardly proclaimed her essence without expectation or reciprocation of mine. As far as she was concerned my uniqueness was as common as the next she. She failed to acknowledge my presence, my sense of style, my inner being that promoted whom I chose to be. Instead, her words of third person prevailed while I, the second person in her space, went unnoticed, unacknowledged and unappreciated.

How does one woman make another woman feel undervalued? Well, she begins with operating from the framework of considering "her" as the objective case of "she." An objective case is a grammatical term indicating a noun or pronoun is an object (dictionary.com).

The result is far from the object of affection, but instead an object to receive negativity, frustration, hate, misplaced anger, oppression and any other emotionally charged abnormality.

You see, beneath the mask, the perceived confidence and the rhetoric, lies a soul damaged from life's occurrences, ransacked with unresolved issues projected upon her, bit by bit until a coping mechanism emerged in the silhouette of a third person, "she." She has been cut, burned and bruised, showing up like scar tissue, the remnants of damage.

Throughout this book the transition of her to she will be explored through Biblical implications and life encounters. It is not intended to place blame but instead to unfold convergent and divergent paths in an effort for reconciliation. It is hoped the utility of capital SHE, aka WISDOM, can be the stepping stones toward healing and ultimately the sustainability of strong, empowered, and mutually beneficial relationships between women.

"Her ways are ways of pleasantness, and all her paths are peace" (Proverbs 3:17). Ruth and Naomi, the power couple as far as a blueprint for mother-in-law and daughter-in-law, strengthened their bond through hardness.

They found themselves yoked after the passing of their commonality, the son of Naomi and husband of Ruth. In all accounts, since no grandchildren existed, it would seem Ruth and Naomi's relationship would have been severed or in contemporary times, first a phone call from time to time, then a card during the holiday season, perhaps an email exchange every now and then, and finally reduced to hitting "like" on a photo from time to time on Facebook. After all, Naomi presented an "out" to both of her daughter in laws. Orpah accepted the invitation.

Ruth rejected it by responding, "Entreat me not to leave you, or to turn back from following you; For wherever you go, I will go; And wherever you lodge, I will lodge; Your people shall be my people, and your God, my God. Where you die, I will die, and there will I be buried. "The LORD do so to me, and more also, if anything but death parts you and me." (Ruth 1:16–17 NKJV). If we were in church, this would be the time when the preacher might ask,

"How many of you have the kind of relationship

with an in-law as did Ruth?" And he or she

might say, "Don't raise your hands, so as to

protect yourself!" This was some deep love and

affection and if I may, I'd like to remove the

context of in-law and instead request we simply

consider it from the perspective of the two

women.

For as far back as I can remember, I've had

loving relationships with women. My induction

came as a result of my mother. My father

passed away when I was five- years-old. My

mother never remarried and furthermore, she

never dated or had a significant other (or

anyone who "spent the night and was referred

to as my uncle"). When I got older, I asked her why and she shared, "I didn't want to train another man." This was spoken in true Altoria fashion; and she meant it. My mother didn't have to balance her love and instead since my brother was 10 years older, we became very close, and she doted on me. She had four sisters, three of whom lived within a 30-minute radius, the fourth 14 hours away, all of whom shared in this affection likely because she was the baby sister, and I was the youngest of all the nieces and nephews. Add and multiply our landlady who was raising three sons, my Sunday School teachers, other members of the church, the ladies at the grocery store, my mom's friends and my school teachers, and you begin to understand when it came to women in my life, mine was reminiscent of a Celie and Nettie Color Purple Reunion on a daily basis.

From my circle, I learned love. I'm fearful because I don't see the duplication of that love as much as I believe we need now as women; and when it is given, there is a cost associated with it. Oftentimes as women, we find ourselves sharing space and there is something that exists in the cosmos which pre-requisites a bond of some sort. I do not suggest agreement with this notion. Simply because we have identical genetic makeup does not make for instant, add water and stir resulting in sisterhood. However, it should make for shared and grounded perspective that guides interaction and deepens empathy such that there remains a desire to desire the best for each other. Somewhere between the "yas" and "honey" we got lost, and I'm terrified the effort our antecedents performed will be dismantled, and not in a good way as likened during the Women of Brewster Place. That narrative told the stories of women living together, striving to thrive in the conditions and situations they were living through. In the end, they came together, from all walks of life, to demolish a wall that represented obstacles, misunderstanding, challenge and defeat. I would suggest through the usage of "she" we are quickly laying the bricks of hatred, jealously, insensitivity, judgment, threat, stupidity and harshness, thus erecting a barrier that will be difficult to overcome. What is even more challenging to consider is this being done in small, yet powerfully driven circles. Their collective voices are blaring, and their ability to destroy booming.

Initially, I thought this to be apparent primarily in reality television. The destruction was somewhat discomforting, but I rationalized the behavior because it was so far removed (or so I thought) from my "reality." However, slowly and methodically, I began to see it rear its ugliness in the workplace, in organizations, on social media, in public, and the kicker, in the House of the Lord! Accordingly, I am convicted to remind us not to forget the poignant words of Lila Watson, "If you've come to help me you're wasting your time, but if you've come because your liberation is tied up with mine, then let us work together." Our inextricable freedom is wrapped within the arms of our sister. Until we unbridle the fabric of our very being, our innermost core, deep in the walls of our soul, we will continue to recycle hate and spew it like heaps of coal upon each other. I recognize the first step to resolution and healing involves admitting there is a problem.

Behind the lashes, the heels, the peplum and the 18 inches, lies numerous disappointments, dreams deferred and unresolved anger as tight as the spanx that she wears. We have masked our pain externally, and celebrate the baddest chick who can cut another first. Instead of our brothers calling this behavior to our attention, many sit by encouraging us to kill each other as likened to a cockfight, betting resources on who will emerge when the smoke is clear. Watch yourself sister, we're going in...

Chapter One:

She (I) Don't Do That!

The Wisdom of SHE: "Wisdom crieth without; she uttereth her voice in the streets." (Proverbs 1:20)

Besides being grammatically damaging, the messaging beyond "she don't do that" is perplexing. Initially, it's hurtful to my ears. It's typically said in response to a request made, either explicit or not. The receiver perceives the request to be belittling, unjustified, unnecessary or beneath them. What is so annoying is it is often referenced in the presence of another sister who may not have the ability or means to reject the action associated with such a definitive declaration. For example, a woman being offered to wear something that is not labeled. Transparently speaking, I was not familiar with a red-bottomed shoe for years. I recently learned not even Ms. O had heard of them until she noticed them on Ms. Tina Turner prior to her retirement. I'm not hating on the decision to rock out Christian Louboutin; but when faced with the reality that some sisters are doing the best they can, holding down a household alone with children depending upon her for their every need, she doesn't deserve shade as a result of what she is wearing in order to make "she" feel validated.

This pattern is problematic and is rooted in a more significant space beyond fashion. "Each of us have sinned and fall short of the glory of

God" (Romans 3:23). We've all allowed our actions to be governed with the spirit of Herodias. She married two of her uncles. She consented her daughter to dance so provocatively, Herodias's husband told the daughter she could have anything she desired.

Upon consultation with her mother, she requested the head of John the Baptist who condemned the behavior and actions of her mother. It appears neither Herodias nor her daughter considered the premise of "not doing that." As opposed to Herodias accepting the wisdom presented to her and possibly altering her lifestyle, she refused instead and set a plan in motion to validate her conduct, much like we do when we echo the sentiment of "she don't do that."

When I hear, "she don't do that" I often wonder, "what exactly does she do?" Does she demonstrate warmth to a sister left in the fragile elements? Does she share how she was delivered from situations and circumstances designed to kill her? Does she encourage the younger generations to value self more than a decision that could alter the course of their lives? Does she honor and respect those who came before her? For that matter, does she honor and respect those who are co-laboring amongst her? Or is she too caught up in projecting a persona void of empathy and self-elected upon a porcelain pedestal destined to crash and burn?

Proverbs 1:20 states, "Wisdom crieth without; she uttereth her voice in the streets." Sadly, what we are hearing in the streets is not that reflective of wisdom, but instead heartless, cruel negativity, planting seeds for our young sisters to opt to behave badly. Stop the madness! Instead, let us consider the reclamation of this phrase for the recovery of our sisters' existence. Are you a part of the mean girls category? Oh, no, She don't do that! Are you finding ways to be manipulative in the workplace? Absolutely not, She don't do that! Are you sleeping with your friend's husband? Certainly not! She don't do that! Are you neglecting your community? Honey, please! She don't do that! Do you crucify yourself because of past decisions and relationships that brought pain? Unequivocally Not! She don't do that!

The path to transition from the original context and meaning of the phrase to the reversion is the utility of SHE, wisdom. Psalm 51:6 reads, "Behold, You desire truth in the inward parts, and in the hidden part, you will make me to know wisdom." Sisters, we've got to have the condition of our hearts repaired.

We each have the opportunity to allow wisdom to act as a stent to ensure that blockage does not persist. Some of us have been afforded directives in wisdom at a very early age, and SHE has been a close confidant, modeled through our mothers, constructed through aunts and teachers, and nurtured through neighbors.

There was even benefit gained from those whom we considered role models in television and film. Others of us had no examples, or even worse, poor examples who projected their pain masked in superior and harmful behavior to us before or without addressing the affairs of their own heart. As human beings living in an imperfect place, riddled with the trouble of the day, we cannot avoid challenge, but we can work on controlling our response. I would suggest beneath the exterior of she lies countless accounts of blockage never quite resolved.

Persons who elect to having a stent placed internally cannot simply rely upon this procedure and return to the way they previously behaved. One of the major alterations must be maintaining an ideal weight. The same is true for when we truly ask God to enter into our hearts. Recognizing it's a process, we must not enable trials, misunderstandings, hurt, disappointment and shortcomings to attach themselves to us like a really cute pair of shoes, but ones that cause inordinate pain... once again, fierce on the outside, but blistered and bruised on the inside. We rid ourselves of baggage or blockage by surrendering to God.

Doing so allows us to live free to make ourselves available for His use. Therefore, when confronted with occasion to respond in a harmful manner to someone, we strengthen our faith, and God can place trouble at our disposal.

Others will hope for a foolish response, while God will confidently say, "She don't do that."

For wisdom will lead and guide where our limited common sense and as the ancestors said, book smarts cease.

What can we do as sisters? We can begin by opening ourselves up and sharing our testimony. When a sister who is being abused overhears you saying, "oh no, she don't do that," tell her why. Tell her it was because you were there before. You know what it feels like to be sharing space and for that matter a marriage with someone who speaks ill of you, who doesn't demonstrate love, who sleeps with the sheets tucked so tightly underneath his body to ensure he doesn't touch you. A person who fails to show love to his daughter, knowing full well a girl's relationship with her father is the first and lasting impression of her relationship with the opposite sex; and used as a measuring stick against every man thereafter. When a sister working a line in a fast food restaurant overhears you saying, "oh no, she don't do that, tell her you haven't always had those letters behind your name. Tell her you couldn't afford to go to school full-time without working to pay your way through. Tell her you used student loan money to pay for childcare and attended class after working a full day at work. Tell her for years you operated on five hours of sleep, and your child didn't have a home cooked meal until your mother came to visit. Tell her you are still paying the debt from earning the degree, but it has landed you in a space to provide options for your children and an occasional vacation with your family, and you wouldn't trade it for the world. As you watch a sister crying over a relationship, and she hears you say, "oh no, she don't do that," tell her your marriage hasn't always been as stable and happy as it outwardly appears. Tell her you felt like leaving within the first 90 days as you do a job. Tell her that it's hard and that it takes the love of Christ to stay. Tell her you make mistakes and you sometimes have to ask forgiveness even when you really feel compelled to be right. When we "fail to do that," fail to express the reality of the reality, we present a false positive to our sisters. However, when we speak the truth we remove barriers that our words and harmful thinking have constructed. In what areas could you be more transparent? At what points on the trajectory can you unpack the baggage you've hidden, and use SHE to uplift she? It is time to reclaim.

Let's alter our approach so we may confidently say, "She did that," and it mean something more than empty words.

#SheWerk:

Pray and ask God to provide a mechanism for sharing a portion of your testimony with another sister whom you believe can benefit. Share with her the entirety of it. Pray and ask God to grant you the ability to be transparent. Offer her a listening ear and encourage her to endure hardness as a good soldier. Find a way to make her smile.

Chapter Two:

She (I'ma) Keeps it 100!

———————————❈———————————

The Wisdom of SHE: "She opens her mouth with wisdom, and the teaching of kindness is on her tongue." (Proverbs 31:26)

I don't know where or when I first heard this statement, but it struck a curious chord. Using my context clues, I understood 100 to be representative of completeness or wholeness; and "I'ma" as an incredibly distorted method of self-referral combined with a state of being; "keep" was straightforward (or so I originally thought, as I'll explain later), but "it" needed unpacking for me. As I listened to this phrase in its utility, I began to understand "it" was a metaphor for a situation, circumstance, a

43

thought, feeling or action when there is perhaps opportunity to act in opposition, but a declarative decision is made instead to maintain a perceptual state of expressed truth.

The more I heard the statement used, I began to wonder. Does the sister making this statement always keep it 100, and if so, what is the cost to those on the receiving end? Does she then have responsibility to adhere to the collateral damage caused as a result of realness? Is there any authenticity in "keeping it 100?" Should we all participate in this practice? What happens when each of us "keeps it 100?" Is anything accomplished? Does "keeping it 100" make us exempt in some capacity thereby serving as a permitted state to act nasty in the moment without apology? May a sister in her forties be allowed to express this sentiment to the same extent as a sister in her twenties? Do we have some people we are expected to keep it 100 with and others whereby it would be considered detrimental to convey the idiom?

Does the state of being truthful require an announcement? Somewhere in that statement is some self-seeking behavior for others to endorse. The concern I have is discretion seems to be non-operational. If expression of truth were indeed an unavoidable state, it would seem it could be done without making the statement. It's like turning on the television to the news, watching the opening credits for the six o'clock news, seeing the anchor sitting behind the desk, and listening to her state, "I'm going to read the news." One is expecting those actions to happen, it's not necessary to state the obvious. So why then state, "I'ma keep it 100?" I would suggest making the statement somehow affirms a pre-disposition to speak before she thinks. For at some juncture, there was opportunity for reflection. Prior to the need to express the statement, there was some withholding of feelings, thoughts, etc. So much so, all of a sudden, an action occurs and one just has to "go in" to pull from that which should have been expressed previously. Further, it comes out nasty because feelings and thoughts have been suppressed. Somehow withholding feelings and becoming overwhelmed allows one to erupt, and making the statement allows others to stamp a seal of approval on the entire situation, even when the approver doesn't have the whole backstory.

In graduate school, I learned about assertive behavior. I learned it was one's ability to express self in a manner that is thoughtful and respectful for others on the receiving end. I fear we are beyond assertive, thriving in the aggressive and destined for rage. Keeping it 100 does not assume consideration for the receiver who is made to feel like 0. There seems to be little regard for the feeling or pain projected when she expresses thoughts, actions, etc., in a manner not culturally responsible for aftermath caused.

I am not suggesting we walk around "keeping" our feelings until we explode into the space of keeping it 100. I'm afraid there aren't quite enough skilled therapists to navigate such an epidemic. Although I would suggest the "keeping" is where the problem originates. For when we do not express ourselves, ask for what we need (not only want), we do a disservice to ourselves, and those around us, and eventually, when time and opportunity meet, we blow up, thus "keeping it 100." Often times, the receiver has nothing to do with our need to express masked authenticity. Instead, they just happen to be the recipient of "time and opportunity" and collect the nastiness that should have been expressed long before in a more thoughtful manner. You know, when bro'man didn't text you back, and you later found out through Facebook on a picture he was tagged in, he really did have opportunity to spend some quality time with you, contrary to the text message he sent? Instead you blow up at her when she asks if you worked on that application for returning to school, telling her she should mind her own business as opposed to trying to run yours.

Most of keeping it 100 is for naught. Even in keeping it 100, there are consequences. We don't often know the difference between keeping it 100 and knowing when to keep our mouths closed. As for me, when I begin to keep it 100, my acceleration is quick. It's best if I don't ever start. For example, in my workplace, I have been upset to the point of keeping it 100 on more than one occasion. However, I have children in college. Shall I keep it 100 and run the risk of being fired and losing the blessing God has afforded to me as a means to undergird their education? The lessons we learn through silence are far more impactful than the mistakes we learn through expression. Job 13:5 reads, "Oh that ye would altogether hold your peace! And it should be your wisdom." There are times when the situation or circumstance before us could be ripe for our words, but we must pray and seek God through the Holy Spirit as to whether it is beneficial for us to speak. We mustn't feel someone is getting away with something because we choose to be silent. Quite the contrary, sometimes God has not yet released us to speak; other times, He is still working on the person we are in conflict with.

Our words may very well circumvent His greater work in not only the situation, but also that person's life. Our words may be the reason a door remains open that God has determined to close.

There is difference between "keeping it 100" when not asked, and simply telling the truth upon request. The Samaritan woman at the well was minding her own business when Jesus, after a long travel experience, asked her for a drink. Immediately, she began to expose her truth. She reminded him of who she was in the cultural framework in comparison to him, and they were not to even communicate with each other, let alone receive something in exchange. Jesus was not concerned with the cultural barriers erected by people; he was interested in her spiritual DNA. Jesus compelled the woman to get her husband, and she responded she did not have a husband. Again, she was being truthful without intention of being harmful. She could have told him that was none of his business, you know, keep it 100, but instead she allowed her truth to make her vulnerable. Jesus told her she was correct, that in fact, she previously had five husbands, and the person she was now with was not her husband, with the implication being he may have belonged to someone else. Instead of keeping it 100 with him yet again, the woman found compassion from Jesus. He knew her attempts to align with many men was instead an attempt to seek something deeper that only salvation could nourish. Her truthfulness, not her nastiness, allowed her to encounter a life altering experience.

A percentage is a number or ratio expressed as a fraction of 100 and is the result of a relationship between two numbers. Let us consider the relationship between she and with whomever she is keeping it 100. While one hundred represents completeness, is she practicing wholeness or wholemess by keeping it 100? In mathematics, sometimes due to inconsistent usage, it is not always clear from the context to what a percentage is relative. In many cases, the projection of realness is in actuality relative to the degree to which she is internally suffering. It's easy to keep it 100.

Anybody can express negativity. The real challenge comes from knowing when to hold your peace, and when to share with the intention of preserving what you have built. The 100 percent could be expressed over time, in smaller percentages, with less damaging effects. That effort requires wisdom. Proverbs 31:26 reads, "She opens her mouth with wisdom, and the teaching of kindness is on her tongue." When wisdom is utilized, there is a decrease in the propensity for nastiness, even "nice nasty" to prevail. However, the "I'ma keep it 100" often results in the finality of the matter, and comes out in such a large and dramatic format, restoration of the relationship (if there truly ever was one) is difficult beyond measure to sustain.

As I write, I am reflecting upon a recent experience whereby a friend said something hurtful to me. If I'd responded the way my flesh directed, it would have gone left and I'm not certain we would be speaking now. Instead, I responded with the Word of God. I recognize the space she is in now. This has been a difficult season for her and she is not ready to receive my 100 or 1 for that matter. Instead, I choose to be led by the Holy Spirit as to if and when I will address the statement she made.

Until then, I will continue to pray for her, but also myself so I am not led into temptation.

I have an idea. The next time we are tempted to keep it 100, let's try reframing the thought and follow the directive of Psalm 100:

> "Make a joyful noise unto the Lord, all ye lands. Serve the Lord with gladness: come before his presence with singing. Know ye that the Lord he is God: it is he that hath made us, and not we ourselves; we are his people, and the sheep of his pasture. Enter into his gates with thanksgiving, and into his courts with praise: be thankful unto him, and bless his name. For the Lord is good; his mercy is everlasting; and his truth endureth to all generations."

Let's keep it 100 by not only stating the Word, but also living the Word. "Faith without works is dead" (James 2: 17), and so is the potential for our relationships without the use of wisdom. I am not suggesting you roll with everything.

Although some situations, just do not dignify a response or energy. God is not keeping a scorecard, and neither must we. What if he kept it 100 and put all of our sin, even our secret sin on blast? The place and space for 100 potentially enacted by God instead masks itself as grace.

Most recently, I was attending a workshop on Hindu culture. The presenter spoke of the concept of karma. Following the event, I was returning to my office with two of my friends and colleagues. Kay inquired, "what then is the equivalent in Christianity for karma?" Our wise friend Dr. AY responded, "Heaven."

Kay and I were focused on the sowing and reaping as the Christian karma, but often we are not made privy to God's punishment to someone who has wronged us.

And, even when we are, rarely does vengeance witnessed feel as good as we imagined. That is because God grants us empathy, the ability to feel and connect with someone else exactly where he or she is presently. Indeed heaven is our reward. If we are so blessed to become an inhabitant, let us recall the strategy to get there steeped it Psalm 100. And that my sister, is keeping it 100.

#SheWerk:

Reflect and determine if you have been a member of the 100 club. If so, create avenues for becoming more transparent in your approach with love. Make a plan to consult God before you "keep it 100" and wait for his direction. If you are not a card-carrying member of the club, consider if you have operated in a secret society capacity, witnessing this bad behavior without interruption or interjection.

How might you become more transparent with God? As God shows you, "you," there will be a decreased tendency to show others "themselves."

Chapter Three:

She's (I'm) Not That Chick

The Wisdom of SHE: "When pride comes, then comes disgrace, but with humility comes wisdom." (Proverbs 11:2)

If pushed hard enough, this phrase may be the sequel to keeping it 100. The interesting shift here is a rejection of a perception that is being incorrectly projected or perceived. For in stating, "I'm not that chick," it's referencing the person on the receiving end has somehow made an assumption that is subject to correction. Perhaps more significant is yet again an expressed comparison of one female to another, with one being superior in some facet to the other. Typically the one that is making the statement is disproportionately better than the other. If we are not that chick, who is?

For many years, chick referred to a baby chicken, but urban slang always does its best work by appropriation. There was a time as I matured, women would go off, in particular at males if referred to as "chick." When the term began to resurface, I thought women were reclaiming it from a negative space; however, I found in its usage, a different case. It remained a derogatory term, even when women were using it against each other. "That chick" represented whom another "chick" did not desire to be confused with. After all, "that chick" acted in ways and demonstrated less flashy behavior. "That chick" perhaps isn't interested in raising her voice, entertaining a brawl nor behaving badly. She on the other hand is down for whatever, whenever and with whomever.

She doesn't desire to be confused with "that chick" because "that chick" allows herself to be for lack of a better phrase, "door matted" whereas she would never allow that.

I would argue "that chick" resides in each of us to a certain extent. Our decision to be vulnerable enough to share her is perhaps the difference in the exhibition; often times hidden, intimidated to come forth with demeaning words, hateful prompts and harmful taunts. I've witnessed the provocation most specifically by women in talking to men, offering a reminder of who she is compared to "that chick." It rarely references something positive. Instead, it's a firm declaration to denounce the other, while upholding self. Proverbs 11:2 reads, "When pride comes, then comes disgrace, but with humility comes wisdom." This verse affirms the inevitable for those who are prideful, while urging us to humble ourselves and be granted wisdom.

As a child growing up on the south side of Chicago during the 1970s in the height of the "Black is Beautiful" movement, I was taught by my family, my neighbors, my teachers and my community to be proud of myself. I was taught to be proud of the contributions of my ancestors, and to be proud of the heritage I possessed despite the color of my skin. Yet, there is a distinction worth noting between being proud and being prideful. Proud is relevant to an accomplishment, task, something tangible, that we may have done or perhaps even someone else. Being prideful is a perpetual exasperated state through which acknowledgement of self supersedes anything or anyone, often to the detriment of others.

Pride involves the projection of disbelief that someone else could actually have something to offer the world in addition to you.

Esther was through positive appropriation, "that chick." If we consider Esther from the original intent of "that chick" she would fit the bill. She was orphaned as a child and although her heritage was of God's chosen people, the Jewish lineage was still persecuted and at that time not in charge. When the King's wife did not agree to a request, he removed her from her position. Esther assumed the role and was Queen. She later learned from her brother of a plot to annihilate the Jewish people. Risking her own life and the life of her people, she shared her true identity with the King. She was serious and concerned about her people, so much so, she was willing to die for their safety, vitality and existence. Sharing her internal state not only saved her life, but the lives of all those connected to her. She could have kept silent and reminded her husband she was not "that chick," but instead, she made a move so bold I would suggest we embrace her in our new revelation as "that chick!"

I want to be that chick who forgives beyond when it hurts. I want to be that chick who remains humble no matter the extent to which God blesses me. I want to be that chick who complements another sister, who upholds her and doesn't believe she is the only one who God blessed to look good in any given situation.

I want to be that chick who shares Godly wisdom when I see another sister going astray in love, and not sit idly by as she crashes and burns. When she doesn't listen and rejects my initial attempts, I want to be that chick who offers solace and restoration, willing to be transparent enough to share the mistakes I've made, and how my life would have been completely altered if not for the grace of God. I want to be that chick who younger chicks think less of being current, but more of being timeless, filled with purpose, love and a desire to see the hand of God and his promises manifest in their lives. I want to be that chick who finds such a deep connection in the man whom God gave me, I have no desire to seek refuge in the one he gave to you. I want to be that chick that refuses to judge another because my greater interest is in my own ability to identify my flaws and my shortcomings, and take them to Christ.

It requires more for me to be "that chick." It is far easier to speak ill of her rather than as

Sister Iyanla Vanzant says, "do my work." We must be careful in our projection moments. What happens when both of us are having an "I'm not that chick" moment? If we both simultaneously bring our baggage can anything good emerge? Whenever I hear a sister say, "I'm not that chick," I actually listen to her admittance to not demonstrating the characteristics of having a teachable spirit. The teachable spirit yields humility and as Proverbs 11:2 affirmed, humility brings forth wisdom. Wisdom, aka SHE will enable the ability to give what she really needs: courage and love. Courage to acknowledge the deficits that have accrued over time; and love to build a repository in exchange for the delinquencies and overdrawn attempts that have festered into a bankrupted life. Chicks have to look out for each other, whether small, large, outgoing or timid, full-grown or in an incubated state. Let's work to get every chick to the other side of the road!

#SheWerk:

Identify examples of characteristics by which you may demonstrate you have a teachable spirit. How might you eradicate any inklings of pride that may exist in your persona? Create a pathway for making a bold move for Christ similar to that of Esther. Keep track of your effort.

Chapter Four:

She (I) Can't Get Along With Other Females

The Wisdom of SHE: "Those who trust in themselves are fools, but those who walk in wisdom are kept safe." (Proverbs 28:26)

When I hear the statement, "she can't get along with other females, a question mark appears in my head. When I inquire and begin to hear the responses, I wish I'd kept my mouth shut.

"Females are a trip, they're jealous, conniving, petty, stupid, catty, overbearing, stuck-up, judgmental, mean-spirited," and any other negative adjective you can conjure. What's sad is the fact men do not only

70

reference such sentiments, but women echo them loudly through a megaphone to drive home the point as well in a footnote capacity. If we as women ever resolve ourselves collectively to seek relationship with each other rather than retaliation, it is unimaginable yet attainable what we have the capacity to birth.

I wonder if and when a female states, "I can't get along with other females" she considers getting along with herself into the equation. I understand the pain experienced through relationship; particularly women, specifically if she hurt you. Yet, as a woman, there is something quite unique about the hurt from another woman. While you may be on the receiving end of taunts, nastiness, expletives, etc., she projects much more significant damage upon herself in the process. Mark 12:21 compels us to love our neighbor as we love ourselves. Just for the record, that includes females.

I have to share, as a teenager, and now as a woman approaching the mid of her life, Eve, was one of the females whom I felt some kind of way about (see next chapter). Each time I experienced my monthly cramping, she came to mind. When I get sick of going to work, she is not far from my thoughts. Something as simple as having a beautiful garden by planting flowers conjures up her image. When I brought my only child into this world, it was done so in pain and I know I screamed in one stream of consciousness my detest for Eve. When I have moments or situations by which I am in conflict with submission to my husband, I give Eve a serious eye and neck roll. Even when I feel as though God's presence is far off, and I've been banished from his presence like a Garden of Eden experience, I can somehow place blame on the woman of all mankind. I guess you might say, she could be a female I couldn't get along with.

As women, we are very much like Eve. Some of us have always had an Eden experience, and others of us have experienced life outside the gate. Just like Eve many of us do not trust God, so it therefore becomes difficult to trust others.

It requires God on the inside of us to see and appreciate the God living inside each of us.

Even more so, with the sister who has yet to invite God to live within her. When we operate from a space of trust and liberation in Christ, we cease from holding our sister in a hostage state, demanding ransom by providing conditions for existence and relationship with us. What I now love about Eve is the fact even though she messed up, God allowed her to give birth, and eventually, he allowed atonement and reconciliation through Christ. Her past did not advert our future. The same continues to be true with our sisters. For whatever she may have done that was indeed hurtful, you are not obligated to hold it against every other female you encounter, nor the one who has been at fault with you. I'm always astounded at how I've witnessed and experienced being in conflict with "one man" and somehow it didn't stop me from being in relationship with another at some point in time. Yet somehow, that grace is not extended to each other as women. We get upset at each other because we have allowed a man (whether partial or full consent) to treat us as my sister Kay refers to as the law of "top, side or in town chick." What do we do? We take it out on the sister who has been tricked as well.

In other words, one negative Eden encounter with "Eve" sets the standard for every woman with the same physiological expression as Eve.

I've been blessed to experience many close relationships with women. Two in particular come to mind. One manifested very early in my life, and the other as I stumbled into early adulthood. Although they were distinctively different, I knew without a doubt they both loved me, as I did them. Within about a five- year period, my communication with both of them ceased. There was no argument or dispute that preceded the silence. I couldn't understand and refused to accept our season of friendship and sisterhood was over. I phoned, texted, emailed, and attempted to visit, but my desperate efforts to connect failed and went unanswered. One of my friends was heavily steeped in developing her marriage, and the other questioning whether to sustain hers. I longed to support them both.

They both supported me through a divorce and both were special and critical to the life of my daughter. They'd shared in so many of my blessings as well as my struggles. Just when my life had finally achieved a consistency of balance, they exited.

As battles emerged in my life, the refuge I'd formerly sought was no longer accessible.

Everyone around me urged me to release them, but I could not. I felt like it was a bad dream I would soon wake up from. Yet when I opened my eyes, I was still captured in the nightmare. I don't know the day or the hour but I decided I would refrain from making any more contact and instead enjoy and celebrate those in my life who remained. Instead of dwelling on what was, I thanked God for loaning them to me. Particularly when God knew I needed them the most. I thanked God for the laughter, tears and joy I experienced with them. I purposed to continue and strengthen those values with other women and relationships God blessed me with.

I pray for my two friends and hope God's perfect will is being made perfect in their lives and their children. I continue to speak well of them, especially around my daughter. My intent is to share the philosophy that undergirds seasons, so she will be more appreciative in the moments, as we don't know how long they will last.

So you were in relationship with another female and she hurt you, disappointed you, caused you some undue pain? Consider looking at her through the lens of God. We walk around failing to consider on any given day, "she" being daughter, sister, wife, mother, aunt, cousin or mistress requires the same love and adoration we so desperately need. Who are we to make accusations? Now every sister may not have equal standing in your life. It would be difficult to assume a sister I sit beside at a conference and elect to have dinner with, may result in the same standing as my college roommate Kieshia whom I've known for over 20 years. However, upon initial contact and introduction, am I willing to explore the possibility of seeking the God in her to connect and commune with the God in me? Or do I measure her against a long, arduous and useless account to every situation by which another woman caused me pain? At that time, you can be certain whatever offense she committed, it did not emerge from a Christ centered space. We all have those momentary lapses, and often what is projected, is actually grounded in deception brimming from the father of lies, and sadly from experiencing fatherlessness. Our earthly fathers play a critical role in helping us to understand who we are. When they are not physically nor emotionally present in our home, we must counter this paradigm by trusting in God.

Consequently, our propensity to damage

others doesn't evaporate overnight. However, as we learn to relinquish our doubt and replace it with our trust in God rather than in a male or female, we can operate openly, without fear or inklings of reciprocity on hold. Proverbs 28:26 reads, "Those who trust in themselves are fools, but those who walk in wisdom are kept safe."

Our wisdom walk through God enables our ability to let our guard down and enjoy fellowship with our sisters without fear of being hurt, without fear of jealously, without fear of retaliation and without fear of abandonment.

Now, if there is harmful, repetitious treatment toward you, no matter the gender, don't subject yourself. That is not fellowship, that's abuse.

Also, there are seasons for relationships with anyone, and instead of belaboring the timing, trust God, be grateful for what you had, and prepare to share that love with someone else.

Sometimes it may return and sometimes it may never be the same; but again we mustn't use our past as a measuring stick for our future.

Getting along with anyone, and in particular women, requires vulnerability, yet the return on investment is far greater than the risk. Women are fierce! We take risks daily, in our workplace, in our communities, in our churches, in our investments, and definitely in our fashion and in our hair. Why not take a risk on another sister?

You might be pleasantly surprised at the

outcome, and if not, just like a great sale, it won't be the last, and sometimes the next one is even better than you expected. The cost to your heart is a lot less.

#SheWerk:

Is there a relationship with another woman that is in need of repair? Are you able to identify the areas by which you have contributed to the problem? How might you extend an olive branch? If you are aware of a breach between two women, how might you allow God to use you as a conduit for restoration? As you continue to build healthy relationships with women, create an opportunity to encourage younger women to do the same.

Chapter Five:
She's (I'm) Feelin' Some Kind of

Way

The Wisdom of SHE: "The perceptive find wisdom in their own front yard; fools look for it everywhere but right here." (Proverbs 17:24)

Talk about a passive aggressive black belted statement! "Some Kind Of Way" is code for a non-positive response that has yet to be fully formatted for expression in one's mind, through one's mouth or actions. It represents a potential heaviness yet to be explored, and serves as a temporary vaccination or a prelude to drama (see next chapter). It puts others on notice that in fact, she could go ham, but she chooses not to in the moment. But instead of keeping feelings and emotions to self, she'll sarcastically operate in the present, letting anyone within a earshot, mile radius overhear a hold is being placed on one's gut, but as soon as processing is completed, its on.

Some kind of way implies on the surface she is not fully connected to the combined conclusion of her emotions and thoughts. However, I would suggest she knows exactly, and chooses in the moment for whatever reason to only share a partial countenance. Is withholding for affect? Is it because there is not an audience? Is more processing required? Is she more comfortable being indirect? Is she being nice nasty? Is it the result of fear?

The Shunammite woman in II Kings, the fourth chapter felt some kind of way. She perceived Elisha to be a Holy Man and she made it her business to be hospitable and generous to him each time he passed through her town. Further, she fed him each time he passed by, so much so, she convinced her husband to build a room for Elisha to rest whenever he passed through.

I wondered if her husband felt some kind of way. Even if he did, he still complied with his wife's request. Gehazi, Elisha's servant was instructed to inquire what if anything could be done for the Shunammite woman. I love the Message's version, for in it, the Shunammite woman responded, "Nothing. I'm secure and satisfied with my family." However, Elisha questioned his servant. Gehazi went on to share, "well, her husband is old, and she has not a son." Elisha acted on what his servant said, and instructed Gehazi to get the woman. There was to our knowledge, no conversation of a desire to be a mother. After all, the woman's husband was old (no disrespect to the brothers). She likely felt some kind of way about the situation. She likely felt some kind of way about the possibility of being a mother. She likely felt some kind of way when questioned or ridiculed about being motherless. She made herself content in doing the work of taking care of her home, family and serving the man of God. Elisha prophesized to the Shunammite woman she would nurse a son within one year.

The Shunammite woman told Elisha, "don't play with me." She felt some kind of way. She likely felt as though she was being set up for disappointment. She was in fact expressing fear. Fear she was being promised something that might not come to be.

There is something to be learned from the Shunammite woman. She did not elect to take the passive aggressive approach even though she was likely justified in feeling some kind of way. Instead, she spoke directly from the innermost parts of her heart. She didn't allow fear to paralyze her faith. Each time we experience a trial in our life, we are positioned to extrapolate wisdom that will assist us when the next trial arrives. Proverbs 17:24 reads, "The perceptive find wisdom in their own front yard; fools look for it everywhere but right here." When we express from our core verbally as, "feeling some kind of way," we permit the enemy to control our antics, projecting our anxiety, pain, disbelief and not our liberation.

We are choosing not to operate in our wisdom. We set the trappings of a future confrontation, when both parties retreat to their respective spaces, complete with ill-informed "shes" positioned to affirm incomplete thoughts channeled into incorrect action. After the Shunammite woman expressed her emotion to Elisha, she didn't refute the prophecy and just as Elisha predicted, she conceived and bore a son.

The child grew and one day complained of a headache to his father who was in the field. He felt some kind of way as well which is why he instructed the boy to go find his mother. The Shunammite mother received her son on her lap and he laid there until noon and died. By this time, I am convinced as a mother, the Shunammite woman was feeling some kind of way. After all, she'd not asked for the son.

Much like we don't ask for disappointment.

However, even if she doubted, she never once said her son could not be saved. "Life and death is in the power of our tongue" (Proverbs 18:21). The Shunammite woman refused to open her mouth and invite the enemy in through passive aggressive speech. Instead, she took action.

As the Shunammite woman gathered her donkey and her servant she told her husband she was going to see the Holy Man. "It's not a holy day" (said the husband). She likely felt some kind of way again, yet she did not waste time getting caught up in things that didn't matter. She chose instead to focus on getting to the man of God who prophesized to her in being blessed with her son. We don't have time to entertain every thought expressed to us. There is no need to feel some kind of way about something, and devise a plan to return to the place of pain to project it on the perpetrator. I once heard Bishop TD Jakes say, "Where would Jesus be without Judas?" We all need someone or something that in the natural thrusts us to the place God desires for us to be in the spiritual. The Shunammite woman had a regimen of preparation for the man of God, Elisha. So must we create a regimen of preparation for Jesus.

When Gehazi and Elisha saw the Shunammite woman coming from afar, Elisha commanded Gehazi to inquire whether it was well. She responded, "It is well." She didn't imply "I'm feeling some kind of way." She spoke what she believed, even though it was yet to come to fruition. Eventually, God through Elisha healed the Shunammite woman's son.

We have access to healing through Jesus.

Each of us feels some kind of way about something, and yet it is in our best interests to connect in a proactive manner with the areas that have caused us pain, disappointment, fear, uncertainty and hopelessness, so statements and actions from others do not have the ability to act as triggers for us. Initially, the triggers reveal surface driven responses, but deep into the foundation, when not properly addressed, triggers exhibit themselves through full-blown trauma. We must find a way to help ourselves with feeling some kind of way. Jesus said, "I am the way, the truth and the life" (John 14:6). Allow him to help unpack the messiness of life and create a portal by which to funnel thoughts into progressive action so you may assume the persona of the Shunammite woman, and not only say, "It is well," but believe it unreservedly in some kind of way, it indeed is!

#SheWerk:

What might God "feel some kind of way" about with you? Classify the areas you have surrendered and are serious about God; as well as those areas where you continue to "play" with him. Create a prayer to ask God to move those challenges you face to the surrendered and serious category.

Chapter Six:

She (I) Don't Do Drama

The Wisdom of SHE: "The mouths of the righteous utter wisdom, and their tongue speak what is just." (Psalm 37:30)

And scene! That phrase is what I want to shout when a sister makes this declaration. Set out the red carpet and grant that sista a golden trophy. Why? Because before you blink, she will conjure up the likes of Cicely, Alfre and Angela as she exhibits exactly what she purports to be immune to. Drama, the postlude to "feelin some kind of way" is considered to be the result of something that could have been easily handled, but instead blown out of proportion. I cannot count how many times I have witnessed such displays and for that matter played a best or supporting role of my own. Perhaps its one's subconscious speaking and our internal state which actually deserves to be heard and loved, yet our external trumps and ushers us into a full display of our talent that could so easily be used for good and not evil.

Drama is not limited to the big screen or in Hollywood or New York. Its borders exceed major cities and some of the most riveting accounts are performed in rural areas, at family reunions, in the workplace, the church and of course social media. A level- headed conversation is considered passé, and exchanged for loud, hurtful, demonstrative exhibition, all the while being touted in a drama free capacity.

While there are a few brothas who have a flare for the dramatic, this is one category where women have our male counterparts beat. It is amped up even more when women are expressing the drama against each other. In the words of Lauryn Hill, "it could all be so simple, but you'd rather make it hard." This sentiment is rooted in truth, because each of us has options before assuming the role and emoting the inspiration of a character through drama. Rarely do we elect to step back and take the time needed to consider all viewpoints and further, make a decision to respond based upon all the evidence, even the consideration of evidence that is unknown. We are so concerned and determined to not be deemed less than or a pushover we pounce and attack unnecessarily, not acknowledging the possibility to operate in self-governance. Self-governance does not come easily. In fact, it results through a process. The initial step is to acknowledge, without being led by the Holy Spirit, you can end up a complete mess.

Drama is defined as the art or activity of performing a role. It is steeped in reality, but the manner by which it manifests is considered overwhelmingly extended. What is even more surprising is she who does not do drama somehow assumes everyone else around her does. Drama presses you to show up for work late, but dares anyone to challenge you on your tardiness. Drama encourages you to show up for a ministry you mentally and spiritually checked out of months ago, but you go so no one will ask you about your physical absence.

Drama supports you in shouting all through the sanctuary, but fail to speak to someone in the restroom. Drama compels us to talk about the women on the reality show and then mimic their behavior during choir rehearsal when you are not chosen to lead the song. Drama thrusts one to act so different on any given day with your husband, he knows not what actress to expect when he reaches home.

We all do drama in one form or another. It's easy to believe we don't simply because we all express it in diverse methodologies. Some of us fall within the comedy category, and get our jabs in through humor and sarcasm. Others are emotionally charged about an issue, complete with melancholy background music playing simultaneously as tears flow, accompanied by gregarious hand movements. Some of us are action-oriented, seeking ways to engage in a physical altercation, or at minimum the façade of one. It is perhaps easy to point a finger at other women, and come short of judgment.

However, how often have we taken matters into our own hands? Have we elected to have a conversation with someone without consulting God and asking him to speak through us? Have we done something in direct opposition against the Word of God all while thinking the infamous, "well God knows my heart?" Have we been intentionally hurtful to someone in retaliation for what they did to us? We are guilty of premeditating our actions without consideration of the consequences. As we mature in Christ, we are less confronted with an immediate situation by which we are not prepared.

Through our prayer time, fasting, reading God's Word and discernment, God has often shown us through the Holy Spirit the unfolding of a "thing." Therein lies time to address an issue in a drama free capacity.

Abigail is a woman who was married to a mean spirited man named Nabal (I Samuel 25). His name is translated to mean fool. After

Samuel died, David spent a great amount of time fleeing from Saul for his life. On one occasion, David was in a space with his men and he protected the property of Nabal. Later, he requested Nabal to share his wealth with he and his followers. Nabal rebuked David by way of one of David's servants. David elected to destroy Nabal and all that he possessed. However, Abigail got word of the destruction her husband Nabal had put into motion. Immediately, without informing her husband, she prepared a feast for David and his followers. When she met David she asked for the life of her husband to be spared. She reminded David of the fact that God blessed him. In return, her life was spared, the life of her husband was spared, and David sent her away with a blessing, and later an invitation to marry. Now, given the fact Nabal likely created conditions for drama to be incubated on a daily basis, Abigail elected not to participate. She did not allow her emotions to overtake her. She utilized wisdom. Psalm 37:30 reads, "The mouths of the righteous utter wisdom, and their tongue speak what is just." Although David and his men could have taken Nabal out, Abigail reminded and reaffirmed David about whom he was in God. She did not allow her past to have rule over her mouth.

This wise decision spared life for Nabal, and likely his servants, and erupted in just a few days later, a new life for her. Romans 8:5-6 tells us "people who are ruled by their desires think only of themselves. Everyone who is ruled by the Holy Spirit thinks about spiritual things. If our minds are ruled by our desires, we will die. But if our minds are ruled by the Spirit, we will have life and peace."

A drama infused environment does not perpetuate peace. It may temporarily produce a sense of release, but in all actuality, the one who operates in drama is in perpetual bondage.

The best dramas are always incredible, but they don't always have a happy ending. Most memorable line as a takeaway, Jesus doesn't do drama and neither should we. Roll the credits.

#SheWerk:

Are you on average the leading lady, the supporting actress or the antagonist in the drama called life? Do you find yourself drawn into situations that continually escalate to a point of no return? How might you allow God to be the ultimate director in all things? Pray and ask God to give you a spirit of discernment or spoiler alert before the show begins. Further if you find you may not be a main character but instead operate as "friend of the theater," ask God to direct your curiosity to where your participation is greatly needed.

Chapter Seven:

She (I) Ain't Got Time for That

The Wisdom of SHE: "For the foolishness of God is wiser than human wisdom, and the weakness of God is stronger than human strength." (I Corinthians 1:25)

She ain't got time for listening to her daughter talk about how she felt at school today while being bullied, because her favorite reality show is getting ready to come on. She ain't got time to listen to her supervisor suggest ways of improving her performance because he doesn't even go to church. She ain't got time to consider dating a married man is wrong, because after all, her husband left her, she is divorced, and it's not her fault his wife can't keep her man under wraps. She ain't got time to listen to one of the church mothers because after all, she's old and things have changed.

She ain't got time to patiently wait for her food and not engage in an altercation after ordering because she already slipped out of work to get her hair done and her absence may be noticeable by now. She ain't, she ain't, and she ain't. Yet, it doesn't stop there and I'd be unfair if I only told one side of Herstory. Let's consider the other.

She ain't got time to listen to God for sound decisions because if he didn't want her to take advantage of an opportunity, he wouldn't have presented it as an option to her. She ain't got time to wait on God to act on the promise he spoke, so instead she takes matters into her own hands. She ain't got time to fall underneath a ministry in church where her covering is, so she replicates her gifts in unfamiliar spaces, unaware of what may be attaching itself to her. She ain't got time to share her testimony with a sister who is hurting and in an identical space, because she is too busy living out her deliverance. Again, she ain't, she ain't, she ain't. Well, what does she have time for? In a world that functions in rapidity, when will she slow down enough to appreciate the quiet space to determine where her energy should be placed, with whom and for how long?

Or in fact, is it simpler to actively avoid what will eventually be revealed as the inevitable?

Waiting on God, and particularly, waiting on the timing of God stirs us to a place where we might be bold enough (but really terrified) to think (forget say), "She ain't got time for that." It implies we are too busy, or rather too anxious to exercise patience. It signals our individual needs or desires trump those whom we find ourselves interacting with. More importantly it drives us to a place of thinking we are wiser than God and he actually needs our assistance in his plan for our lives.

God promised Abraham he would be the father of many nations. But as the years passed, Abraham and his wife Sarah began to doubt God's promise. Sarah urged Abraham to begin the process of nation building by taking her servant Hagar as his mistress. Hagar bore Abraham a son. The relationship and the child angered Sarah. As more years passed, the Lord spoke to Abraham through a visitor and decreed that within a year, his wife Sarah would bare a son. Sarah overheard the conversation and laughed. I can only imagine Sarah's laughter translating to "I ain't got time for that!" She was 90-years-old and barren. Her husband was 100 and biologically speaking, neither of them were in a position to be considered eligible for procreation. But God. Just as what was prophesized, but more importantly, what was promised, Sarah bore a son named Isaac, thus beginning the lineage God spoke to then Abram, decades earlier.

Just like Sarah, we feel the need to take matters into our own hands. Often times, like Sarah, we too are disappointed with our handiwork.

Waiting on God is learned through a process, and instead of seeing God through timing, we mistakenly charge the enemy as being the culprit for delay. God can move in a situation or on a promise at any time he desires. However, we are not always positioned or prepared for the promise. We must create the condition for the promise to be fulfilled. That condition emerges through our personal purification process; and that is what we ain't got time for! I Corinthians 1:25 reads, "For the foolishness of God is wiser than human wisdom, and the weakness of God is stronger than human strength." Even when we believe God doesn't know what he is doing, and moving slower (or what may appear as not at all) than what we expect, or what he has promised, even in what may be perceived as his foolishness, is wiser than the wisdom he has imparted to us. It is further difficult to imagine God's weakness. When I witness evil in the world, I have been guilty of feeling as though the enemy is "winning" in comparison to God. I must remind myself that the Word of God tells us the enemy must ask for permission for all he does, and nothing occurs without God's knowledge.

Therefore, even our perceived weakness of God is stronger than the strength he has provided to us.

God ain't got time as well. He ain't got time for us to play, especially when there is work to be done. We are his tangible extension in the earth, and often we are guilty of being complacent when he has called us to active duty. He ain't got time for us to try every passing fad when his Holy Word which has existed for centuries remains a viable guide for our daily living. He ain't got time for us to walk around in bondage, when he directed his only begotten son to take on our sin, be crucified and resurrected for our liberty. He ain't got time for us to be frivolous with the gifts he has deposited within us for the building of his kingdom. He ain't got time for us to judge when we are not equipped nor endorsed to carry out a responsibility akin to only him. He ain't got time for us to be legalistic and religious to the point where we deter others from accepting Christ as their personal savior. He ain't got time for us to act as though salvation was only extended to those who attend a certain sec of the church, when the only requirement is to believe. He ain't, he ain't, and he ain't!

Even through all of "God's ain'ts" he still loves us unconditionally. He embraces us when we fail to embrace she. He loves us while we secretly (and sometimes openly) hope for the demise of she. He blesses us while we think she needs to suffer a little longer and wait just like we did. She has his attention, as do we.

And as stated previously, the utility of SHE will allow us to maneuver through life and all it comprises, and ensure she does as well. The she that is another sister, and the she who resides in us that we often treat as an extension of ourselves as opposed to the very nature, is actually our core, and the center of self. I'm so glad He ain't gave up on all of us! Let's make it our business to make time to be about our father's business, while we still have time.

#SheWerk:

What dream have you tucked away? The Word of God tells us "faith without works is dead" (James 2:20). What needs to be resurrected? In addition to seeking God and asking for clarity and the wherewithal to bring your dream to fruition, ask God for accountability through another sister to ensure you don't give up and pursue your passion.

Sheclusion

Ruth and Naomi emerged from distinct spaces.

They were culturally different. They were different ages. The original bond that brought them together was severed, and yet, they found solace in one another and pushed beyond perceived societal limitations and perspectives in order to develop a mutually beneficial relationship. Their love for each other emerged as a result of pain. It is the perfect illustration of God's ability to give us what we need even when we are unable or unwilling to acknowledge it. The same can be true in contemporary times with our sister.

We too emerge from distinct spaces. We are culturally different. We come in vast sizes, shapes and hues. Often the bond that brings us together is obvious; school, ministry, work, sorority, community engagement, church, hobbies, etc. Other times, we are brought face to face by painful circumstances, sickness, divorce, and infidelity, verbal and/or physical altercations. Just as in the case of Ruth and Naomi, it is not for us to determine how God elects to bless us. When we make ourselves available and seek God, he will always direct us on a path that means us well. We want to be blessed of God, and yet we must be open to the manner by which he chooses to bless us; even someone not of our own choosing. We must begin to seek God in each other.

When we are unable to find evidence of him operating in our sister, we must choose to love them as God loves us – despite our imperfections, flaws, temptations, personal defeats and countless outpourings of grace.

Before we can love another, we must love ourselves. When on a plane, we are instructed to take care of self before assisting others. We each have our personal "she" who may be called upon to act out, in a moment, in a twinkling of an eye. She must be self-disciplined so she does not suffocate the plan God has ordained. Once she is under control and self-governed, she can compliment without expecting a compliment back. She can see past the outer appearance of a sister and seek the core. She can be excited for her blessings without jealously. She can appreciate and celebrate in her season of blessings. When she does this, the tendency to project the insecurity is halted and the materialization of love is overwhelming; in other words, she is led by SHE.

In mathematical terms "x" represents an independent variable of unknown value.

Further, "x" signifies multiplication. In genetics, females are comprised of "xx" chromosomes.

As women, we are independent and unknown, and therefore, we must take double the effort to get to know each other; understand each other's strengths, our desires, our fears, and our Achilles' heel, without holding it against each other. As the ancestors would say, "the conclusion of the matter" is that every one of us must matter to each other. She is counting on you. No matter the presentation, just as Ruth said to Naomi, "entreat her not to leave you!" SHE will ensure she endures. SHE always has and always will!

Stephanie Helms Pickett's life has been reflected by Ephesians 3:20, "Now to him who is able to do exceedingly, abundantly, above all that we can ask or think, according to the power that worketh within us."

Reared in Chicago by her mom, her biggest inspiration, Stephanie fell in love with writing at an early age.

She holds a Bachelor's degree in Radio & Television Broadcasting from Southern Illinois University at Carbondale; and a Master's and Doctorate degree in Higher Education Administration from North Carolina State University.

She has previously worked at Bennett College for Women, the North Carolina Department of Instruction, Durham Public School System, Meredith College, Barton College, North Carolina State University and Clark Atlanta University.

Stephanie serves as the Coordinator of the Anointed Soles Dance Ministry at Wake Chapel Church in Raleigh North Carolina under the leadership of Pastor J. Jasper Wilkins Jr. She is a member of the Chapel Hill/Carrboro Graduate

Chapter of Alpha Kappa Alpha Sorority, Incorporated.

She is the Director of Assessment & Professional Development Programs in the Division of Student Affairs at Duke University and Visiting Professor in the Program in Education.

In August 2009 the Lord blessed her union to Charles Pickett, Sr,. Their blended family includes two teenagers, Charles Pickett Jr. (20), Niani, (19) and one dog, Diamond Star. They reside in Raleigh, North Carolina.

She recently published her first book, "Later Never Came Until Now," which explores academic disciplines through the Word of God and personal narratives.